PINK GIN · ANTIBES · PINK MARTINI

DECAR · RAMOS GIN FIZZ · JEWEL OF

IN AND SIN · NI

RLATIVE MAR NI

LIME MARTINI · JUPITER COCKTAIL

· GOLD MARTINI · BALI HIGHBALL

COCKTAIL · TASMANIAN TWISTER

CKTAIL · JOCKEY CLUB · RENDEZVOUS

TAIL · COCO CHANEL · BEAUTY SPOT

HORN · TYPHOON · LEE MILLER'S

YALE · · · · · · · · · · · · · · ·

Mini Bar *Gin*

Mini Bar Gin

by MITTIE HELLMICH

photographs by Frankie Frankeny

CHRONICLE BOOKS

SAN FRANCISCO

A huge thanks to the fabulously creative project manager Mary Wruck for her savvy attention to detail, and to the meticulous copy editor Jonathan Kauffman. And a special thanks to Hudson Pierce-Rhoads, Geoffrey Rhoads, and Rick Van Oel.—MH

Library of Congress Cataloging-in-Publication Data available.

ISBN 10: 0-8118-5424-8
ISBN 13: 978-0-8118-5424-5

Manufactured in China.

Drink styling by Alison Richmond
Designed by Hallie Overman, Brooklyn, New York

From Frankie: Thanks to Pamela Geismar and Leslie Jonath.

Distributed in Canada by Raincoast Books
9050 Shaughnessy Street
Vancouver, British Columbia V6P 6E5

10 9 8 7 6 5 4 3 2 1

Chronicle Books LLC
680 Second Street
San Francisco, California 94107

www.chroniclebooks.com

Table of Contents

Introduction

GIN IS THE QUINTESSENTIAL COCKTAIL LIQUOR, one that has inspired many classic cocktails, from the Martini and the Negroni to slings, fizzes, rickeys, and collinses. Historically infamous, gin has swung between extremes of taste and class, from the dangerous swill produced by London gin houses to the glamorous spirit made fashionable by the literary set and Hollywood during the golden age of cocktails.

The origins of gin are rooted in juniper-based medicinal cures that were first distilled by Italian monks around 1150. But we can raise our martini glass to the Dutch for refining the distillation process and making the apothecary's tonic into a recreational tipple. By the 1650s, the Dutch were producing *genever* (which the word *gin* is derived from), a drinkable spirit with an intense juniper bouquet.

English mercenaries who aided the Dutch during the Thirty Years' War (1618–48) brought home more than a few bottles of "Dutch courage," but England's thorny love affair with the spirit really began with William III, a Dutch aristocrat who assumed the British throne in 1689. He brought along his preference for Holland gin, and soon the ports of Bristol, Plymouth, and London became major distilling centers. Imbibed from the fashionable Banqueting House at Hampton Court Palace (dubbed the "gin temple") to the slums of London, gin became the perfect numbing distraction from reality, and by the early eighteenth century, the infamous "gin shops" took root, producing unregulated and dangerously bad distillates. By 1769, gin's reputation was restored by Alexander Gordon, who was licensed to distill high-quality gin.

The popularity of gin in America can be followed from the turn-of-the-century bar scene, strictly for sophisticated urbanites, through the decadent 1920s, and Prohibition era's home-distilled "bathtub" gin, producing harsh gins that harkened back to the infamous London gin shops. Franklin Roosevelt, a Martini aficionado, ushered in the first "legal" Martini in 1933, further perpetuating the already popular cult of the Martini, which eventually evolved into the maximum-dryness fetish of the 1950s and '60s.

DISTILLING GIN

Gin starts out like vodka, as a colorless, light-bodied spirit distilled from grain (wheat or rye) or cane (molasses). It parts company with vodka once the base spirit is flavored. Gin is distilled in column stills, producing a clean, light-bodied, high-proof spirit, and is then redistilled with botanical flavorings, usually in an Old World pot still. The quality of gin varies depending on the raw ingredients, the purity of the added water, and the method of distillation.

Beyond the usual flavors of juniper and coriander, distillers craft distinctive, complex gins by adding their own combination of botanicals—from clove, lemon, and orange rind to licorice, anise, and cardamom among others. The best-quality gins are redistilled with these flavorings, which are suspended within the still and vaporized into the spirit for complexity. By comparison, mass-market brands infuse the botanicals by soaking them in the base spirit and then redistilling the infused spirit. The lowest-end brands, known as "compound gins," simply add essences and extracts to a neutral spirit.

GIN TYPES

When people refer to gin, they usually mean London dry gin, which is most often used in cocktails. However, there is a wide spectrum of styles of gin available, from pungent Holland gins to softer American dry gins, with each distiller striving to produce subtle aromatic differences.

London dry gin, classically English in style, is the traditional dry gin, light and aromatic. It is the most popular style on the market. From the mildly perfumed to the pungent, these bone-dry gins lack the sweetness of old-style Old Tom gin and are great for both mixed drinks and martinis. Similar to London dry gin, Plymouth gin (produced only in the city of Plymouth) is intensely fragrant, fuller bodied, and very dry. It makes a perfectly acceptable Martini.

Old Tom gin is one of the few remaining examples of old-style gin popular in eighteenth-century England, a slightly sweetened type similar to Holland's *oude* genever.

Holland still makes its classic genever, a Dutch-style gin that is highly aromatic with intense juniper flavor. Genever is produced in three styles, from dry, lighter bodied *jonge* (young) genevers, to pungent, slightly sweet *oude* (old style), as well as *Korenwijn*, a wood-aged genever. These are best served neat or over ice rather than used in mixed drinks.

Dry gins made in the United States tend to be softer and less flavorful than London dry gins and are best suited for mixed drinks. France produces a few gins that fall between the intensely pungent and softer, dry varieties. The newer "second generation" gins, which jump on the flavored vodka craze, are infused with a broad spectrum of aromatic botanicals such as orange, clove, vanilla, mixed citrus, and pear. Some leave the juniper taste so far behind that we must ask, is this technically still a gin?

GIN MIXOLOGY

Now, when it comes down to stirring and shaking, the aromatic characteristics of gin concord so marvelously with just about any ingredient, from juices to liqueurs and vermouth, that gin is a luxuriant spirit for mixed drinks. A moderate or cheaper brand is perfectly suitable for multi-ingredient mixed drinks, but a premium gin can be fully appreciated when prepared in a Martini or Gin and Tonic.

Whatever your tastes, from the sophisticated Negroni and Orange Blossom to the lively Singapore Sling, you'll find that this compilation of gin drinks offers a wide spectrum of mixologically mastered classics, contemporary concoctions, and innovative cocktails, sure to inspire shaking and pouring with style.

Salut and enjoy!

Glassware, Tools, and Terminology

Glassware plays an important role in the much-ritualized cocktail experience. A well-chilled vessel visually entices us with the promise of refreshment, with the right glass adding elegance to even the simplest drink. Glasses come in an endless variety of designs, styles, and colors, but when it comes to setting up your home bar, your repertoire of glassware doesn't have to be extensive to be stylishly appropriate and proficiently functional. A few basic styles—cocktail glasses, highball glasses, old-fashioned and double old-fashioned glasses, champagne flutes, and wineglasses—will see you beautifully through a multitude of drinks.

ESSENTIAL BAR TOOLS

Whether you have a swank bar setup in your favorite enter-taining room or an area set aside in the kitchen, you don't need all the high-tech gadgets and gizmos to put together a well-functioning home bar. All you need are the essential bar tools to see you through just about any mixological occasion. You may already have the typical kitchen tools you need: a sharp paring knife for cutting fruit and garnishes, a cutting board for cutting fruit, a bar towel, a good corkscrew and bottle opener, and measuring spoons and cups. To these you may want to add a few of the basic bar tools: a blender with a high-caliber motor, a citrus juicer, a cocktail shaker or a mixing pitcher and stirring rod, a bar spoon, a jigger, an ice bucket and tongs, and, of course, a few cocktail picks and swizzle sticks.

To dash, muddle, top, or float: That is the question. When you want clarification on what exactly that all means or what it means to have a drink served up, neat, straight, or on the rocks, this miniglossary of frequently used bar terms will assist you in navigating bar talk.

· Chaser · The beverage you drink immediately after you have downed anything alcoholic, usually a shot. Typical chasers are beer, club soda, and juice.

· Dash · Either a shake from a bitters bottle or the equivalent of approximately ⅛ teaspoon.

· Dry · A term meaning "not sweet," used either in reference to some wines or to describe nonsweet spirits or cocktails, such as a Dry Martini, which uses dry vermouth rather than sweet vermouth.

· Float · This describes the technique of slowly pouring a small amount of spirit (usually a liqueur or cream) over the surface of a drink so that it floats, or sits atop another liquid without mixing. The customary technique is to slowly pour the liquid over the back of a spoon.

· Highball · The main characteristics of a highball drink are that it has two ingredients—one spirit and one mixer, usually carbonated, poured into a tall, narrow glass filled with ice (the shape of the glass helps to contain the carbonation)—and that it can be mixed quickly. The tall, but narrower Collins glass is a frequent alternative to the highball glass.

· Lowball · A lowball is any drink served with ice in a short glass, such as an old-fashioned glass.

· Muddle · A technique that involves using a small wooden "muddler" or spoon to mash fruits or herbs in the bottom of a glass, usually together with bitters or sugar, to release their aromatic flavors.

· Neat · Describes a single spirit or liqueur served in a glass "straight up"—enjoyed on its own, unchilled, and without ice, water, or any other ingredients.

· Neutral Spirit · A spirit distilled from grain to produce a virtually tasteless, colorless alcohol that is 95.5 percent ABV (alcohol by volume) and is used as a base for spirits such as vodka or gin or for blending with straight whiskeys or other spirits and liqueurs.

· On the Rocks · A term used to describe any liquor or mixed drink served over ice—the "rocks" being ice cubes—as opposed to a drink served "up" (without ice).

· Perfect · A term used to describe specific cocktails that contain equal parts dry and sweet vermouth, as in a Perfect Manhattan or Perfect Martini.

· Pousse-café · Literally translated as the "coffee-pusher" (and pronounced *poos-caf-FAY*), this after-dinner drink features colorful strata of liqueurs, syrups, spirits, and creams in a stemmed glass. The multiple layers—as many as seven—are artfully floated one on top of another so that each stratum remains separate. The heaviest liquid goes in first, the lightest is added last.

· Proof · A legal measurement of the alcoholic strength of a spirit. In the United States, proof is calculated thusly: 1 degree of proof equals 0.5 percent ABV (alcohol by volume). Therefore, a spirit labeled "80 proof" is 40 percent ABV, a 100-proof spirit is 50 percent ABV, and so on.

· Splash · A small amount that can fall anywhere between a dash and about an ounce, depending on who's doing the splashing.

· Straight · This term describes a spirit served without any other liquor or mixers, either poured into a chilled glass or over ice, occasionally with the addition of a splash of club soda or water.

· Top or Top Off · A term used by bartenders to describe the act of pouring the last ingredient into a drink, usually club soda or ginger ale, filling to the top of the glass. Also used to describe filling a beer mug from a tap.

· Up · Describes a drink served without ice in a cocktail glass. Usually the drink is shaken in a cocktail shaker and strained "up" into a chilled cocktail glass, as opposed to "on the rocks," which means served over ice.

simple

· Easy-to-prepare cocktails with four ingredients or less ·

Gin Rickey

COCKTAIL LORE HAS CONNECTED THE ORIGINS of this fizzy classic to Shoemaker's, a bar in Washington, D.C. Shoemaker's was frequented by lobbyists in the 1890s, and specifically one Colonel Joe Rickey, for whom the drink was concocted. Similar to a collins or a fizz (both which use lemon juice), the Rickey is traditionally made with the juice of half a lime and, refreshingly, without any sugar.

Pour the gin and lime juice into an ice-filled highball glass. Top with club soda and stir gently. Squeeze the lime wedge over the drink, and drop it in.

2 ounces gin

1 ounce fresh lime juice

3 to 5 ounces chilled club soda

Lime wedge

Gibson

THE SIGNATURE CHARACTERISTIC OF THE GIBSON is a pickled-onion garnish. Though the drink resembles the Martini (you know, the one with the olive), the Gibson has a following all its own. It was originally made with equal parts gin and dry vermouth and a maraschino cherry! The modern Gibson was created in the 1940s at the Players Club in Manhattan for American artist Charles Dana Gibson.

2 ounces gin
¼ ounce dry vermouth
Pearl cocktail onion

Stir the gin and vermouth in a mixing glass with ice. Strain into a chilled cocktail glass. Garnish with the onion.

· Variation · For an ultra-dry Gibson, pour 2 ounces chilled dry gin into a chilled cocktail glass misted with an atomizer spray of Noilly Prat dry vermouth.

Gin and Tonic

SOMEWHERE IN THE TROPICS AROUND THE EARLY 1900S, this thirst-quenching drink was first concocted by a nameless Englishman who brilliantly splashed just the right amount of quinine-laced sparkling water into his glass of gin. Once another anonymous genius introduced a squeeze of lime, the Gin and Tonic became a wildly popular drink served in all the best tropical hotels, and naturally caught on as a summertime libation. The proportions of gin to tonic are crucial for a perfectly balanced G&T experience (of course, that balance is purely subjective). This recipe is a good place to start; many prefer theirs with a lot of fresh lime squeezed in.

2 ounces good-quality gin
4 ounces chilled tonic water
1 or 2 lime wedges

Pour the gin and tonic water into an ice-filled old-fashioned glass. Stir well. Squeeze the lime wedges over the drink, and drop them in.

Pink Gin

HERE IS A COCKTAIL "REMEDY" FROM THE EARLY DAYS of the British Empire in India. Pink Gin was popular with British officers for its purported ability to soothe the stomach. Often referred to as Gin and Bitters, and similar to a Gin Cocktail with orange bitters, this cocktail was a favorite of writer Ian Fleming, of James Bond fame. The classic method is to rinse a sherry glass with the bitters first, and then to add the chilled gin. It is traditionally served with a glass of water on the side. For a Gin and Pink, simply add 5 ounces tonic water and serve over ice in a highball glass, with the lemon twist.

Pour the bitters into a chilled sherry or cocktail glass, and swirl to coat the glass. Discard the excess. Pour in the gin. Garnish with the lemon twist.

4 to 5 dashes Angostura or Peychaud's bitters
2½ ounces chilled gin
Lemon twist

Antibes

SEND YOUR SENSES TO THE SOUTH OF FRANCE with this elegant cocktail, which perfectly balances the complex flavors of gin, tart grapefruit juice, and aromatic Bénédictine, a Cognac-based herbal liqueur that adds a honeyed sweetness to the drink. Known as the world's oldest liqueur, Bénédictine was named after the Bénédictine monks of the Abbey of Fécamp in Normandy, who formulated it around 1510. The exact formula may be cloaked in secrecy, but we do know that the liqueur is made with as many as 75 botanicals, including citrus peel, honey, basil, rosemary, and sage.

Shake the liquid ingredients vigorously with ice. Strain into an ice-filled old-fashioned glass, and garnish with the orange slice.

1 ½ ounces gin
½ ounce Bénédictine
2 ounces fresh grapefruit juice
Orange slice

Pink Martini

AS MUCH AS I ENJOY A WELL-MADE MARTINI, once the hot summer months arrive I crave something a little more balmy. This little pink refresher gets the tropical treatment with just the right amount of guava nectar and fresh-squeezed orange juice to accent the botanical notes of gin beautifully.

2 ounces good-quality gin
½ ounce guava nectar
½ ounce fresh orange juice
Orange twist

Shake the liquid ingredients vigorously with ice. Strain into a chilled cocktail glass. Run the orange peel around the rim, twist it over the drink, and drop it in.

Gimlet

THE GIMLET WAS ORIGINALLY CONCEIVED when sailors in the British navy combined their rations of gin and lime juice as a remedy for avoiding scurvy. The name was inspired by a "gimlet," the corkscrew-like device used to tap into the kegs of lime juice. As the Gimlet evolved, the key citrus ingredient became sweetened Rose's lime juice, introduced by Lauchlin Rose of Scotland. This classic recipe, from the 1930s Savoy Hotel bar, is reflective of the popular proportions of the time, which were further glamorized by writer Raymond Chandler in *The Long Goodbye*. His character, detective Philip Marlowe, pontificates on his favorite cocktail: "A real gimlet is half gin and half Rose's lime juice and nothing else." For those who desire a more contemporary ratio, stir 2½ ounces gin together with ½ ounce Rose's lime juice, or if you prefer fresh lime juice instead of Rose's, ½ ounce simple syrup (recipe follows) or 1 teaspoon superfine sugar will be needed. Many also enjoy drinking a Gimlet through a sugar rim, the glass first moistened with lime juice.

1 ¼ ounces gin
1 ¼ ounces Rose's lime juice
Lime wedge

Stir the gin and lime juice in a mixing glass with ice. Strain into a chilled cocktail glass. Squeeze the lime wedge into the drink.

· Basic Simple Syrup · Also known as SUGAR SYRUP, this is an essential ingredient in many drinks, as it requires no dissolving or excessive stirring to incorporate, unlike granulated sugar. Makes 2 cups.

1 cup water	2 cups sugar

In a small saucepan, bring the water to a boil. Remove the pan from the heat and add the sugar. Stir until the sugar is completely dissolved. Cool completely before using or refrigerating. Pour into a clean glass jar, cap tightly, and store (indefinitely) in the refrigerator until needed.

Costa Del Sol

FIND THE WARMTH OF THE SPANISH MEDITERRANEAN IN THIS aromatic cocktail, in which apricot brandy and the brandied orange notes of Cointreau give junipery gin a decidedly sunny disposition.

Shake the ingredients vigorously with ice. Strain into a chilled cocktail glass.	2 ounces gin 1 ounce Cointreau 1 ounce apricot brandy

savvy

· Essential recipes for every bartender ·

Chelsea Sidecar

ALSO KNOWN AS THE CHELSEA HOTEL OR GIN SIDECAR, this is a signature drink from the Chelsea Hotel in New York. A variation on the classic Sidecar, the Chelsea version replaces the Cognac with gin, and Sidecar aficionados will be happy to know that it's equally as fabulous and refined. Nor is it far off from the Maiden's Prayer—a classic that appeals to contemporary tastes. Simply add ½ ounce orange juice to the consortium.

Rub the rim of a chilled cocktail glass with the lemon peel. Shake the liquid ingredients vigorously with ice. Strain into a chilled cocktail glass. Garnish with the lemon twist.

Lemon twist
2 ounces gin
¾ ounce Cointreau
½ ounce fresh lemon juice

Ramos Gin Fizz

THE RAMOS BROTHERS USHERED THIS CLASSY COCKTAIL INTO popularity in the 1890s, when it became the signature libation of the New Orleans Imperial Cabinet Saloon. This Gulf Coast variation on the Gin Fizz calls for the brothers' essential ingredient—orange flower water, which can be found in most specialty food shops. Tradition insists the Ramos Gin Fizz be well shaken in a cocktail shaker for about 5 minutes (held with a bar towel) to completely froth and blend the egg white; however, you may prefer the more expedient modern option of using a blender. Use raw egg at your discretion, or substitute pasteurized egg.

2 ounces gin

1 ounce fresh lemon juice

½ ounce fresh lime juice

1 teaspoon vanilla extract

2 to 3 dashes orange flower water (see recipe introduction)

1 egg white (optional)

1½ ounces cream

1 tablespoon superfine sugar

2 to 4 ounces chilled club soda

Lemon slice

Shake all ingredients except the club soda and lemon slice vigorously with ice for 3 to 4 minutes. Strain into a chilled highball glass. Top with club soda and stir gently. Garnish with the lemon slice.

Jewel of the Nile

THIS SHIMMERING, POTENT ELIXIR IS PACKED full of botanical bling. Melding gin with both green and yellow Chartreuse, two fine herbal liqueurs made from more than 130 herbs and plants, gives this jewel of a drink an intensely aromatic flavor. Chartreuse was created in the sixteenth century by Carthusian monks in a monastery in Grenoble, France, a silent order that still makes the liqueur and helps keep the recipe secret. Green Chartreuse is an intense 110 proof and yellow Chartreuse is "only" 80 proof, sweeter, lighter, and slightly minty. Brilliantly hued, they lend an unearthly glow to this appealing cocktail.

Stir the ingredients in a mixing glass with ice. Strain into a chilled cocktail glass.

1 ½ ounces gin
½ ounce green Chartreuse
½ ounce yellow Chartreuse

Delmonico Number 1

A SWANK CLASSIC THAT PREDATES PROHIBITION, this perfectly balanced concoction was the house cocktail at New York's famous Delmonico Restaurant. Traditionally served in a Delmonico glass (similar to a sour glass), it can be garnished with either an orange or a lemon twist.

Shake the liquid ingredients vigorously with ice. Strain into a chilled cocktail glass. Garnish with the orange twist.

1 ounce gin
½ ounce brandy (or Cognac)
½ ounce dry vermouth
½ ounce sweet vermouth
2 dashes Angostura bitters
Orange twist

Gin and Sin

STRAIGHT FROM THE 1950s, this tony tipple conjures up cocktail hour in twinkling low-lit lounge style. Later versions became less classically refined and martini-like, and if you insist on taking the juicier, more contemporary route, add another ¾ ounce of orange juice and ¼ ounce of lemon juice.

2 ounces gin
¼ ounce fresh orange juice
¼ ounce fresh lemon juice
2 dashes grenadine

Stir the ingredients in a mixing glass with ice. Strain into a chilled cocktail glass.

Martinez

ONE OF THE ASSUMED PREDECESSORS TO THE MARTINI,
the Martinez is a much sweeter concoction than the modern-
dry Martini. The original, first created in California during
the Gold Rush of the 1850s, was made with equal parts sweet
vermouth and Old Tom gin (a sweeter gin), and was usually
sweetened further with maraschino or orange liqueur.

Shake the ingredients vigorously
with ice. Strain into a chilled
cocktail glass.

2 ounces Old Tom gin
½ ounce sweet vermouth
¼ ounce maraschino liqueur
Dash of orange bitters

Negroni

A CLASSIC COCKTAIL THAT EVOKES LANGUOROUS ITALIAN SUMMERS and café-hopping—only natural, given that the key ingredient is Campari, the popular Italian aperitif, which lends the drink a vibrant scarlet hue. Around the turn of the century, as the story goes, Florentine Count Camillo Negroni had the vision to request a splash of gin be added to his Americano (half Campari, half Italian sweet vermouth, with enough club soda for some fizz). The result was a brilliant alchemic triangulation of gin, bitter Campari, and sweet vermouth. The Negroni is traditionally served over ice to slightly dilute its intensity, and a refreshing splash of club soda is optional. The drink is equally enjoyable when shaken and served up. The classic recipe dictates equal parts gin, Campari, and sweet vermouth, but there are many variations.

1 ounce gin
1 ounce Campari
1 ounce sweet vermouth
2 to 3 ounces chilled club soda (optional)
Orange slice

Shake the gin, Campari, and vermouth vigorously with ice. Strain into an ice-filled highball glass. Top with club soda, if desired. Garnish with the orange slice.

· Variations · For a PUNT E MES NEGRONI, substitute ½ ounce Punt e Mes for the Campari.

For a NEGRONI COCKTAIL, shake the gin, Campari, and vermouth, omitting the club soda, and strain into a chilled cocktail glass. Garnish with an orange twist instead of the orange slice.

For a DIRTY DICK'S DOWNFALL (after Nixon), a lighter, martini-like version, use 2 ounces gin, ½ ounce dry vermouth, and ½ ounce Campari. Garnish with a lemon twist.

Flamingo

AS THE NAME SUGGESTS, THIS DRINK IS INDEED FLAMINGO PINK, compliments of the grenadine. But the saving grace is tart lime juice, which wonderfully counterbalances all that apricot brandy and grenadine sweetness.

Shake the ingredients vigorously with ice. Strain into a chilled cocktail glass.	1 ½ ounces gin ½ ounce apricot brandy ½ ounce fresh lime juice ¼ ounce grenadine

· Variation · For a classic PARADISE, substitute orange juice for the lime juice and drop the grenadine.

The Martini

The Martini, a symbol of pure alchemy and glamour, is structured on the perfect balance between the juniper berries in gin and the herbal qualities of vermouth. The myths describing its moment of creation are legion—from "Professor" Jerry Thomas of San Francisco's Occidental Hotel, who purportedly created the drink for a miner on his way to the town of Martinez, to a late-1800s English invention named after the Martini-Henry rifle, or even to Martini di Arma di Traggi, a bartender at New York's Knickerbocker Hotel in 1910.

One thing we know for sure—the original ratio of equal parts London dry gin and Noilly Prat dry French vermouth, with a dash of orange bitters, is not dry enough for modern tastes. The proportions of a 1930s Martini became progressively more dry, finally reaching the absurdly dry extreme of straight chilled gin by the 1950s (which, in actuality, is called a Naked Martini). For purists, however, whatever the dryness ratio—even if it's misting the glass with Noilly Prat or infusing the olive with dry vermouth—it must have vermouth to be a Martini.

W. Somerset Maugham, a firm believer that Martinis should never be shaken, poetically stated, "Martinis should always be stirred, not shaken, so that the molecules lie sensuously on top of each other." But purists such as Maugham have contention from the more contemporary camp, following the spy who made it oh-so-stylish to shake.

The Superlative Martini

THE TRADITIONAL DRY VERMOUTH FOR THE MARTINI is Noilly Prat, although any dry vermouth will suffice, but a premium-quality gin is the only guarantee of a perfect Martini. Store both the gin and the glasses in the freezer for the ideal icy coldness. Stir your liquid ingredients gently with cracked ice or ice cubes in a glass martini pitcher until the glass turns frosty, and strain into a chilled cocktail glass. Garnish with either an olive or a lemon peel twisted over the drink to diffuse the tart, bitter oil from the rind into the drink.

Stir the gin and vermouth in a mixing glass with ice. Strain into a chilled cocktail glass. Run the lemon peel around the rim, twist it over the drink, and drop it in (or simply drop in the olive).

2 ounces gin
½ ounce dry vermouth
Lemon twist (or green cocktail olive)

· More variations on the classic Martini · For a DRY MARTINI,
reduce the dry vermouth to ¼ ounce.

For an EXTRA-DRY (OR VERY DRY) MARTINI, reduce the dry
vermouth to ½ teaspoon or less. Whether the vermouth
is administered via a dash, an eyedropper, or an atomizer, or
is swirled around the glass just to coat it with a vaguely
vermouthian flavor, this version can be as dry as you like it.

For a FINO MARTINI, add 2 dashes fino sherry.

For a SMOKY MARTINI, add ¼ ounce single-malt scotch.

For a PERFECT MARTINI, make with equal parts (½ ounce each)
sweet and dry vermouth, and garnish with an orange slice.

For a BRONX COCKTAIL, (invented in 1906 at the Waldorf Astoria),
add ¾ ounce orange juice to a Perfect Martini.

Dirty Martini

THIS POPULAR BRINE-INFUSED VARIATION ON THE CLASSIC MARTINI
was a favorite of Franklin Delano Roosevelt, who historically
served one up to Joseph Stalin in 1943.

Stir the liquid ingredients in a
mixing glass with ice. Strain into a
chilled cocktail glass. Garnish
with the olive.

2 ounces gin
½ ounce extra-dry vermouth
½ ounce brine from
cocktail olives
Green cocktail olive

Tom Collins

THE EPITOME OF 1950S SUBURBIA, this classic drink was actually created in the mid-1800s by John Collins, barman at Limmer's Hotel in London, as a variation on his Holland gin–based John Collins cocktail. He named the original drink after the slightly sweet Old Tom gin, but a later version made with London dry gin became much more popular. Tom Collinses caught on in America after World War I vets brought them home from Europe.

2 ounces gin
1 ounce lemon juice
½ ounce simple syrup
   (page 25) or 1 teaspoon
   superfine sugar
3 ounces chilled club soda
Lemon slice
Maraschino cherry

Pour the gin, lemon juice, and simple syrup into an ice-filled collins glass. Top with club soda and stir gently. Garnish with the lemon slice and maraschino cherry.

· Variations · For a TEX COLLINS, substitute 3 ounces fresh grapefruit juice and 1 tablespoon honey for the lemon juice and simple syrup.

For a RASPBERRY COLLINS, add ¾ ounce crème de framboise and 3 ounces raspberry puree, and garnish with a few raspberries.

RASPBERRY COLLINS ▶▶

Singapore Sling

THIS INTERNATIONAL HIT WAS CREATED at the Raffles Hotel in Singapore in 1915 by bartender Ngiam Tong Boon. The immense popularity of this famous drink inspired a multitude of variations throughout the Pacific, making it difficult to actually pin down the original recipe. The one that seems to prevail is a concoction of gin, cherry brandy, lime juice, and Bénédictine. Other variations call for a splash of soda or for the cherry brandy to be floated on top. This recipe encompasses all the best aspects of a great Singapore Sling.

Shake all of the liquid ingredients but the club soda vigorously with ice. Strain into an ice-filled highball glass or double old-fashioned glass. Top with club soda and stir gently. Garnish with the pineapple, orange slice, and maraschino cherry.

1 ½ ounces gin
¾ ounce cherry brandy
¾ ounce Bénédictine
¾ ounce Cointreau
1 ounce fresh orange juice
¾ ounce fresh lime juice
2 to 3 ounces chilled club soda
Pineapple wedge
Orange slice
Maraschino cherry

· sophisticated ·

· A little more work but definitely worth the effort ·

Key Lime Martini

WHAT COULD BE BETTER THAN A GREAT KEY LIME PIE? A Key Lime Martini, of course! Inspired by the dessert, I concocted this sweet-tart elixir from those tiny, tart limes hailing from the Florida Keys and mellowed its puckeriness with sweet, vanilla-orange Tuaca liqueur.

Rub the rim of a chilled cocktail glass with the lime wedge and rim with sugar. Shake the liquid ingredients vigorously with ice. Strain into the prepared glass. Float the lime wheel on top.

Lime wedge

Sugar

1 ½ ounces gin

1 ounce Tuaca

1 ounce fresh Key lime or other lime juice

½ ounce simple syrup (page 25) or 1 teaspoon superfine sugar

Thinly sliced lime wheel

Jupiter Cocktail

YOU DON'T HAVE TO WAIT UNTIL JUPITER ALIGNS WITH MARS to cast spells of seduction when you have Parfait Amour in hand. This lavender-hued liqueur, aromatic with the flavors of violet and orange, is said to have potent aphrodisiacal qualities (a reputation acquired from its use in refined Parisian brothels). It makes for a perfectly perfumed concoction that is ideally enjoyed with your paramour under a starlit night.

1 ½ ounces gin
½ ounce dry vermouth
¼ ounce Parfait Amour
¼ ounce fresh orange juice

Shake the ingredients vigorously with ice. Strain into a chilled cocktail glass.

Orange Blossom

THIS ARTFUL COCKTAIL HAS GONE THROUGH A FEW TRANSMUTATIONS, from the Waldorf Astoria's version made with equal parts gin, orange juice, and sweet vermouth to a basic Screwdriver-like highball containing equal parts gin and orange juice (also known as an Adirondack). Here is the classic version, which keeps resurfacing for good reason.

Shake the liquid ingredients vigorously with ice. Strain into an ice-filled old-fashioned glass. Garnish with the orange slice.

1 ½ ounces gin
1 ½ ounces fresh orange juice
¼ ounce Cointreau
1 to 2 dashes orange flower water (see page 28)
Orange slice

Capri Cocktail

ONE SIP, AND YOU'LL SWEAR YOU'RE HEARING VESPAS ZIPPING BY.
This refreshingly fruity, tangy cocktail integrates the essential
Italian ingredient, limoncello liqueur, into a tropical fusion
of flavors that includes a whisper of orgeat syrup. It's sure to
shanghai your senses straight to a breezy summer café on
the isle of Capri.

Shake the ingredients vigorously
with ice. Strain into a chilled
cocktail glass.

1 ½ ounces gin
½ ounce limoncello
¼ ounce peach schnapps
1 ounce fresh grapefruit juice
1 ounce mango juice
Dash of orgeat (or almond-
    flavored syrup)

Gold Martini

THIS COCKTAIL DEFIES ALL THE RULES. A provocative martini so full of complexity and contradiction, from the potent blending of divergent spirits to the exotically intriguing addition of fresh ginger, that it must be sipped slowly—it's pure gold, baby!

1 ½ ounces gin
½ ounce citron vodka
1 ounce Cointreau
¼ ounce brandy
3 to 4 thin slices fresh ginger
Candied ginger slice

Shake all the ingredients except the candied ginger vigorously with ice. Strain into a chilled cocktail glass. Garnish with the candied ginger slice.

Bali Highball

A WAVE OF INSPIRATION CAN ROLL IN AT ANY TIME AND FROM the strangest of places. For instance, Bing Crosby was crooning "Bali Hai" in the background when I conjured up this lush, tropical elixir. Enlisting a bottle of real pomegranate syrup, which was crying out to be elevated to a more refined plane, I engineered this effervescent ambrosia, reminiscent of a sling. It is fragrantly sweetened by guava and pomegranate syrup (the ingredient that the ersatz red-colored bottled corn syrup we call grenadine is based on), with the zing of fresh lime juice to keep the sweetness in check.

1 ½ ounces gin
2 ounces guava nectar
½ ounce fresh lime juice
1 ounce pomegranate syrup
3 to 4 ounces chilled club soda
Lime wheel
Orange blossom (or other edible flower)

Shake the gin, guava nectar, lime juice, and pomegranate syrup vigorously with ice. Strain into an ice-filled highball glass. Top with club soda. Garnish with the lime wheel and orange blossom.

Death in the Gulfstream

ERNEST HEMINGWAY, SEEMINGLY ALWAYS IN NEED OF A GOOD HANGOVER REMEDY, created this drink, although there is a bit of speculation as to the exact time and place—some say the Hotel Ritz in London in 1922, others, Key West in 1937. Nevertheless, we do know that Hemingway's preference was for the more intensely pungent genever, but we'll never tell if you use a good-quality London dry gin instead. Either way, this tipple is indeed, according to its maker, "tart and bitter—reviving and refreshing."

Pour the gin and lime juice into an ice-filled highball glass. Add the sugar and bitters and stir to combine. Twist the lime peel spiral over the drink, and drop it in.

2 ounces gin
1½ ounces fresh lime juice
Pinch of superfine sugar
3 to 4 splashes Angostura bitters
Lime peel spiral

Kyoto Cocktail

THE APPROACH MAY BE STYLISHLY MINIMAL, but when fragrant gin, herbal vermouth, and sweet melon liqueur come together, these Oriental and Occidental flavors cavort to infuse this cocktail with aromatic abundance.

Shake the ingredients vigorously with ice. Strain into a chilled cocktail glass.

1 ½ ounces gin
½ ounce dry vermouth
½ ounce melon liqueur
Dash of fresh lemon juice

· Variation · For an EVERGREEN, top with a splash of blue curaçao, and garnish with a maraschino cherry.

Tasmanian Twister

WHEN SUMMER PATIO SOIREES ARE IN NEED of an enlivening cocktail, I like to tart up one of my favorites, the classic Negroni, with a splash of fresh pink grapefruit juice. Despite the crazy title, the balance between the herbal notes of gin Campari and the sweet vermouth together with fresh juice is pure sophistication.

1 ½ ounces gin
½ ounce Campari
½ ounce sweet vermouth
1 ounce fresh pink grapefruit juice
Orange twist

Shake the liquid ingredients vigorously with ice. Strain into a chilled cocktail glass. Twist the orange peel over the drink, and drop it in.

Vesper Martini

CONJURED STRAIGHT FROM IAN FLEMING'S CASINO ROYALE, this infamous martini was James Bond's cocktail of choice. It was named after Vesper Lynd, Bond's doomed double-agent girlfriend. The potent cocktail appropriately calls for Russian vodka, symbolic of Vesper Lynd's allegiance to the Russians, and is served with an orange twist to complement the Lillet, a delicious replacement for vermouth. The drink is served in Bond's preferred glass, a champagne coupe, and of course, it is shaken, not stirred.

Shake the liquid ingredients vigorously with ice. Strain into a champagne coupe or chilled cocktail glass. Twist the orange peel over the drink, and drop it in.

2 ounces gin
¾ ounce Russian vodka
⅓ ounce Lillet Blanc
Large orange twist (or a traditional lemon twist)

sensual

· Luxurious yumminess for your mouth ·

Orchid

AN EXOTIC FLOWER IN A GLASS, the Orchid melds juniper and citrus, then decadently perfumes the duo with the subtle almond flavor of crème de noyaux, the vanilla-orange tones of Tuaca, and violet-orange flavors from Parfait Amour.

Rub the rim of a chilled cocktail glass with the lemon wedge and rim with sugar. Shake the liquid ingredients vigorously with ice. Strain into the prepared glass.

Lemon wedge
Sugar
2 ounces gin
1 ounce crème de noyaux
½ ounce Tuaca
½ ounce Parfait Amour
1 ounce fresh lemon juice

Parisian Cocktail

QUINTESSENTIALLY FRENCH, this cocktail beautifully balances equal amounts of the botanical flavors of gin, sweet black currant liqueur, and herbaceous Noilly Prat, the bone-dry French vermouth.

1 ounce gin
1 ounce crème de cassis
1 ounce Noilly Prat dry vermouth

Stir the ingredients in a mixing glass with ice. Strain into a chilled cocktail glass.

Jockey Club

NAMED AFTER THE AMERICAN JOCKEY CLUB, this cocktail has come a long way from the basic gin-and-bitters drink served at the Waldorf Astoria. By the 1930s, the Savoy Hotel in London was serving up this embellished version.

2 ounces gin
¼ ounce crème de noyaux
¼ ounce white crème de cacao
¼ ounce fresh lemon juice
Dash of orange bitters

Shake the ingredients vigorously with ice. Strain into a chilled cocktail glass.

PARISIAN COCKTAIL ▸▸

Rendezvous

THERE'S NO GUARANTEE THIS ENGAGING CUTIE will encourage any clandestine meetings, but the intriguing play of junipery gin, dry morello-cherry-flavored kirsch, and slightly bitter, orange-scented Campari is sure to spark something.

Shake the liquid ingredients vigorously with ice. Strain into a chilled cocktail glass. Twist the lemon peel over the drink, and drop it in.

1 ½ ounces gin
½ ounce kirsch
½ ounce Campari
Lemon twist

Arcadia

FAR FROM SIMPLISTIC, this elixir poetically melds the juniper of gin and the anise of Galliano with the balmy flavors of banana and grapefruit to induce sheer contentment.

Shake the ingredients vigorously with ice. Strain into a chilled cocktail glass.

1 ½ ounces gin
½ ounce Galliano
½ ounce crème de banane
½ ounce fresh grapefruit juice

Alexander

ALTHOUGH THE BRANDY VERSION has become more popular, the original Alexander recipe (which dates back to the 1920s) contains gin, which lends a botanically fragrant note and is equally as tasty.

1 ounce gin
¾ ounce white crème de cacao
¾ ounce heavy cream
Pinch of freshly grated nutmeg

Shake the liquid ingredients vigorously with ice. Strain into a chilled cocktail glass, and sprinkle with nutmeg.

· Variation · For an AVALANCHE, substitute brown crème de cacao for the white.

Passion Cocktail

A COCKTAIL FANTASY: You find yourself on a tropical island with a bottle of gin and no vermouth in sight. Forced to improvise, you add a little passion fruit juice…and once you get back to civilization, you happily find Alizé de France, a Cognac-based liqueur flavored with tart passion fruit, to transport you back to your bliss-filled paradise.

Coat a chilled cocktail glass with the liqueur and discard. Stir the gin in a mixing glass with ice. Strain into the prepared glass. Garnish with the lemon peel spiral.

¼ ounce Alizé de France passion fruit liqueur

2 ounces Bombay Sapphire gin

Lemon peel spiral

· Variation · For a classic ORIENTAL COCKTAIL, add another ¾ ounce Alizé de France and ⅔ ounce limoncello.

Coco Chanel

WHY THIS CHIC DRINK DOESN'T INCLUDE CRÈME DE COCOA, as the name suggests, is a mystery. Nonetheless, it is one of those timelessly delicious combinations of rich coffee-flavored Kahlúa and cream. Here the pair meld beautifully with the subtle fragrance of gin. A lovely choice for late-evening sipping.

1 ounce gin
1 ounce Kahlúa
1 ounce heavy cream

Shake the ingredients vigorously with ice. Strain into a chilled cocktail glass.

Beauty Spot

A RICH, CHOCOLATY AFTER-DINNER DRINK complete with a sexy beauty spot—as well as egg white, which must be well shaken to froth up delectably. Use raw egg at your discretion, or substitute pasteurized egg.

2 ounces gin
½ ounce white crème de cacao
1 egg white
½ teaspoon grenadine

Shake the gin, crème de cacao, and egg white vigorously with ice. Strain into a chilled cocktail glass. Drop the grenadine in the center of the drink; do not stir.

· stimulating ·

· Caffeinated and fizzy drinks for a fun buzz ·

French 75

THIS ELEGANT COCKTAIL, purportedly named after a French-made 75mm howitzer used in World War I, was popular at Harry's New York Bar in Paris. Originally made with Cognac and served over ice, the drink is now a gin-based cocktail frequently served up in a champagne flute. It has also been known under the alias of Diamond Fizz.

Shake the gin, lemon juice, and sugar with ice, and strain into an ice-filled collins glass or a chilled champagne flute. Slowly top with champagne. Garnish with the orange peel spiral.

1 ounce gin
½ ounce fresh lemon juice
1 teaspoon sugar
5 ounces chilled brut champagne
Orange peel spiral

Ritz 75

STRAIGHT FROM THE RITZ HOTEL BAR IN PARIS comes this sunny, citrusy variation of the classic French 75, a great alternative to serve at brunch in place of the usual Mimosa.

Shake all ingredients but the champagne vigorously with ice. Strain into an ice-filled collins glass or a chilled champagne flute, and slowly top with champagne.

½ ounce gin
½ ounce fresh lemon juice
½ ounce fresh mandarin juice
1 teaspoon sugar
4 ounces chilled brut champagne

· Other variations on the French 75 · For a SOIXANTE-NEUF, omit the sugar, and add a lemon twist.

For a KING'S PEG, omit the sugar and lemon juice.

For a FRENCH 69, add ¼ ounce Pernod.

For a FLYING COCKTAIL, add ¼ ounce Cointreau.

Gin Fizz

THERE ARE MANY FIZZY DRINKS based on the refreshing combination of gin and citrus juice, but this Prohibition-era classic is a highball that really hits the spot. The main difference between a fizz and a collins is that in a fizz, the ingredients are traditionally shaken to help dissolve the sugar and get a good froth going before the splash of club soda is added.

2 ounces gin
1 ounce fresh lemon juice
1 teaspoon sugar
2 to 3 ounces chilled
    club soda

Shake the gin, lemon juice, and sugar vigorously with ice. Strain into an ice-filled highball glass. Top with club soda and stir gently.

· Variations · For a SILVER FIZZ, add an egg white (see recipe introduction, page 28).

For a GOLDEN FIZZ, add an egg yolk (see recipe introduction, page 28).

For an IMPERIAL FIZZ, add 1 ounce lime juice.

For a ROYAL GIN FIZZ, use champagne in place of the club soda.

For a GRAND ROYAL FIZZ, add 1 teaspoon maraschino liqueur, 1 ounce orange juice, and ¼ ounce half-and-half.

Foghorn

THE WALDORF ASTORIA, revered center of the cocktail universe at the turn of the last century, served up this concoction, only it was made with the sweeter Old Tom gin and called a Marguerite. This updated version uses London dry gin for an effervescent thirst-quencher.

Pour the gin and lime juice into an ice-filled old-fashioned glass. Top with ginger ale and stir gently. Squeeze the lime wedge over the drink, and drop it in.

2 ounces gin
½ ounce fresh lime juice
3 to 5 ounces chilled ginger ale or ginger beer
Lime wedge

· Variations · For a DOLOMINT, add 1 ounce Galliano, top with chilled club soda in place of the ginger ale, and garnish with a lime wedge and a mint sprig.

For a DRAGONFLY (also known as PROHIBITION CHAMPAGNE), squeeze the lime wedge only, omitting the lime juice.

For a LEAP FROG (basically a GIN BUCK), substitute 2 ounces lemon juice for the lime juice.

Typhoon

AT FIRST GLANCE, this cocktail may seem elegant and refined, but within the bubbly is a monsoon of flavors and a potency that suggests you hang on to that palm tree before you have another.

1 ounce gin
Dash of Pernod
½ ounce fresh lime juice
4 ounces chilled champagne
Lime twist

Shake the gin, Pernod, and lime juice vigorously with ice. Strain into an ice-filled highball glass. Slowly top with champagne, and stir gently. Garnish with the lime twist.

Lee Miller's Frobisher

THIS 1940S-ERA CHAMPAGNE COCKTAIL of classic composition is named after the equally stylish photographer Lee Miller, infamous as muse and model for the surrealist artist Man Ray.

2 ounces gin
Dash of Angostura bitters
4 to 6 ounces chilled
   champagne
Lemon twist

Pour the gin and bitters into an ice-filled highball glass. Slowly add the champagne, stirring gently. Run the lemon peel around the rim, twist it over the drink, and drop it in.

Pall Mall

CALL THIS YOUR SECOND-WIND MARTINI. This merry charmer is a popular classic from the 1930s and has just enough pepperminty crème de menthe to refresh and refuel.

Stir the ingredients in a mixing glass with ice. Strain into a chilled cocktail glass.	1 ½ ounces gin ½ ounce dry vermouth ½ ounce sweet vermouth 1 teaspoon white crème de menthe Dash of orange bitters

Juniper Royale

THIS DRINK TAKES THE ROYAL TREATMENT even further by gilding the juniper flavor with fruit juices and a blush of pink grenadine for a bubbly elixir of pure pleasure.

Shake all ingredients but the champagne vigorously with ice. Strain into a chilled champagne flute, and slowly top with champagne.	1 ounce gin ½ ounce fresh orange juice ½ ounce cranberry juice Dash of grenadine 3 to 5 ounces chilled champagne

Index

Liquid Measurements

BAR SPOON	½ ounce
1 teaspoon	⅙ ounce
1 tablespoon	½ ounce
2 tablespoons (PONY)	1 ounce
3 tablespoons (JIGGER)	1½ ounces

¼ cup	2 ounces
⅓ cup	3 ounces
½ cup	4 ounces
⅔ cup	5 ounces
¾ cup	6 ounces
1 cup	8 ounces
1 pint	16 ounces
1 quart	32 ounces
750-ml bottle	25.4 ounces
1-liter bottle	33.8 ounces

1 medium lemon	3 tablespoons juice
1 medium lime	2 tablespoons juice
1 medium orange	⅓ cup juice

GIN RICKEY · GIBSON · GIN AND TON

GIMLET · COSTA DEL SOL · CHELSEA

THE NILE · DELMONICO NUMBER 1

FLAMINGO · THE MARTINI · THE SU

TOM COLLINS · SINGAPORE SLING ·

ORANGE BLOSSOM · CAPRI COCKT

DEATH IN THE GULFSTREAM · KY

VESPER MARTINI · ORCHID · PARISIAN

ARCADIA · ALEXANDER · PASSION CO

FRENCH 75 · RITZ 75 · GIN FIZZ · I

FROBISHER · PALL MALL · JUNIPER